PICTURE PUZZLES

What's Different?

Play these other great puzzle books by USA TODAY:

USA TODAY Sudoku
USA TODAY Everyday Sudoku
USA TODAY Crossword
USA TODAY Logic
USA TODAY Sudoku X & Mini Sudoku
USA TODAY Word Roundup & Word Search
USA TODAY Word Play
USA TODAY Everyday Logic
USA TODAY Jumbo Puzzle Book

PICTURE PUZZLES
What's Different?

---

100 PUZZLES
from The Nation's No. 1 Newspaper

**Andrews McMeel
Publishing®**

Kansas City · Sydney · London

Andrews McMeel Publishing, LLC
an Andrews McMeel Universal company
1130 Walnut Street, Kansas City, Missouri 64106

www.andrewsmcmeel.com

14 15 16 17 18 WKT 10 9 8 7 6 5 4

ISBN: 978-0-7407-7854-4

puzzles.usatoday.com

ATTENTION: SCHOOLS AND BUSINESSES
Andrews McMeel books are available at quantity discounts with bulk purchase for educational, business, or sales promotional use. For information, please e-mail the Andrews McMeel Publishing Special Sales Department:
specialsales@amuniversal.com

Introduction

Tailgating, the 4th of July, Mardi Gras, Thanksgiving dinner, burger joints, golf outings, BBQ, fly-fishing, knitting—these American events and pastimes, along with glorious wildlife and exotic destinations, make the perfect scenes for our picture puzzle brain teasers. Most of the puzzles included here are our version of spot-the-difference games. We've also included in this collection a few picture scrambles and some "Which one is different?" puzzles.

A few tips for solving these puzzles: As you compare the two seemingly identical pictures, view each photo as a grid. Start at a corner and compare that section to the same section of the opposite picture. Continue working through the pictures section by section, carefully comparing every element. For the scrambles, we'll give you one section for starters. Survey the edges of the starter section, then look among the other sections for the piece that would align on one or more edges. Find that next piece and build from there; you'll be able to solve even the most difficult scrambles.

Happy puzzling!

ELEMENTARY

Ah, the Spa

Relax—finding these differences should be effortless.

Happy 4th!

Have a ball . . .

Panda Express

This giant cutie will find a bit less to eat in one of these photos. Can you tell which is different?

1

2

3

4

5

6

At Home
Please don't eat the daisy.

Double Decker

Looks like Big Ben could use a hand.

Anybody Home?

Watch your step.

○ ○ ○ ○ ○ ○ ○ | **8** CHANGES

Crafty Critters

Eye spy something amiss.

Hello, Birdie

Perch on this puzzle for a few minutes and you'll easily spot the eight changes.

Purse Panic

Put this purse profusion back in order and you'll have this one in the bag.

Don't Rock the Boat

Choose carefully if you take out one of these boats. You might be going in circles.

Koala Canteen

We've interrupted this koala's mealtime in the gum tree. Quickly find the picture that doesn't match, then move on so he can eat without an audience.

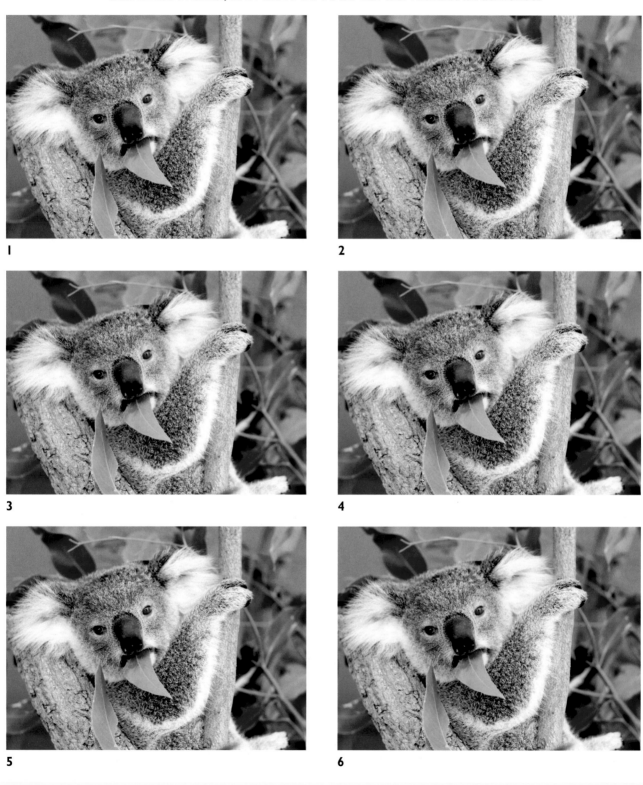

1

2

3

4

5

6

Blowin' in the Wind

Breeze on through this easy puzzle and find the seven alterations we've made to this idyllic setting.

Paws for Reflection

It would be grrrreat if you could spot all the differences.

Ready, Set, Go

Five of these starting-line shots are identical. Can you find the one that is off track?

1

2

3

4

5

6

Pool Party

These toys seem to be doing more than keeping the kids afloat.

Garden Variety

Five of these spring scenes are the same.
Dig a little deeper to find the one that's different.

1

2

3

4

5

6

Splish Splash

Make way for ducklings.

Steady . . . Steady . . . Don't Fall!

This pyramid likely will last about as long as it takes you to find the eight differences.

Three Buddies

Which one of these precious pictures does not purrfectly match the others?

1

2

3

4

5

6

Play on Through

Come on, dear, hit it close.

Don't Budgie Me!

It should be easy to *spot* these differences.

Mixed Signals

These signal flags have gotten mixed up. Put the patterns back in order before someone gets the wrong message.

Senior Moment

You'll deserve a medal, too, when you solve this puzzle.

Soccer Saturday

These tikes can't wait to get the game underway. Can you find all the changes before the whistle blows?

○ ○ ○ ○ ○ ○ ○ | **8** CHANGES

A Cherry on Top

Inflation appears to have rocked this retro diner.

A HAPPY MEDIUM

All Dressed Up

Beads and baubles and pom-poms, oh my!

Baked Goodies

Hey, Cookie, this puzzle is a piece of cake.

Defending the Pirate Booty

What's so harrrd about this?

Vacation—All We Ever Wanted

Five of these sunny scenes are identical.
Can you find the one that's a shade different?

1

2

3

4

5

6

We're Bowled Over

Is there a kingpin in this frame?

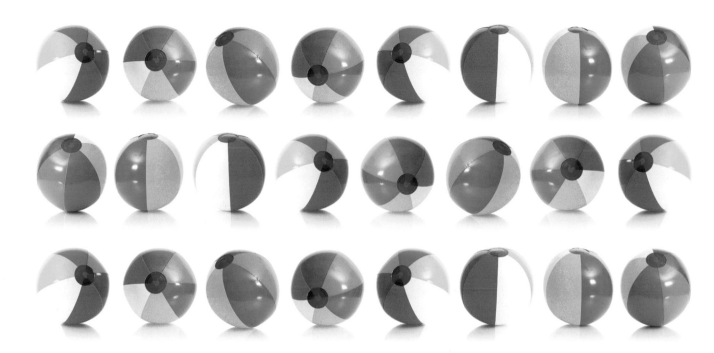

Beach Bonanza

You'll have a ball with this one.

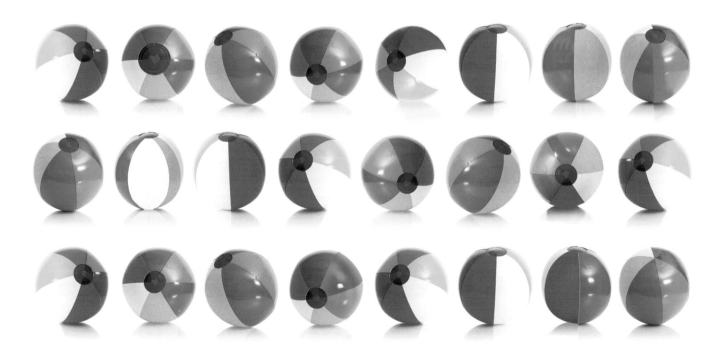

Buried Treasure Chest

X marks the spot.

Chocolate Heaven

Something nutty is going on here.

Poolside Paraphernalia

Things will go swimmingly once you dip into this puzzle—just ducky, in fact.

Patient Penguins

Do you have the patience to find the one
image that doesn't match the others?

1

2

3

4

5

6

Flower Power

These lovely blooms must be well fed!

Dinner Time
Looks like a pooch has been into the kibble.

Tie One On . . .

A scarf, that is.

Mini Me

Take the bull by the horns and solve this puzzle.

Hope You're Hungry

The sushi appears to be multiplying.

Go Fly a Kite

But first, find the differences.

Stinky Cheese

Hold your nose and open your eyes to find the differences between these cheesy pictures.

Will It Go 'Round in Circles?

Stop! We want to get off and find the differences.

Don't Be Koi

You know you can easily put this pond back within its banks.

Laptop Loungers

Hmmm. Wonder what has these ladies so bugged?

Tailgate U.S.A.

No quarterback sneak in this parking lot party, but something sneaky did happen to this picture.

Sweet Tooth

Don't blow a raspberry at us. We'll get our just desserts when you
find the ten changes we've made to these sweet tarts.

Primary Colors

Do you have a painter's eye? Brush up on your technique and find
the ten changes we've made to this colorful canvas.

Say, "Cheese!"

We think the carnival magician has brought some trickery to this scene.

All Smiles

Can you keep this family happy by finding the one
picture that doesn't match the others?

1

2

3

4

5

6

Pizza Party

There should be plenty of Parm for these pies.

Happy, Smiling Faces

Everyone should know the multiplication tables, but you don't need them to solve this puzzle.

Shoe Fetish

Which pair doesn't quite match up?

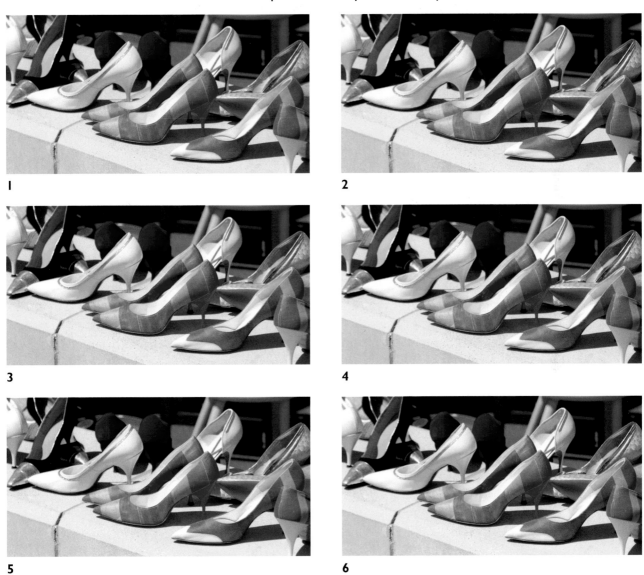

1

2

3

4

5

6

Hindsight

Don't jump to conclusions; this course is harder than it looks.

Slurp

We've taken a straw poll and it's unanimous—there's something suspicious going on here.

○○○○○○○○○○○○ | 12 CHANGES

Shop 'Til You Drop

We hope she has a new pair of earrings in one of those bags.

Ding-Dong

These goblins are getting tricked *and* treated.

Oh, Buoy, Lobster!

This puzzle may look deceptively easy, but don't be roped into that line of thinking.

○ ○ ○ ○ ○ ○ ○ ○ ○ ○ | **10** CHANGES

Manatee Migration

Is that what's going on in this picture or is another slow mover the star of this show?

Fall Feast

We've added extra trimmings to this Thanksgiving dinner. Invite the whole family to help solve the puzzle.

USA TODAY.

Where Old Surfboards Go to Die

Gidget could solve this puzzle. Can you?

The Good Life

Tee up your eagle eye and find the changes we've made to this serene setting.

Stormy Seas

This boat has hit some choppy waters. You may need all hands on deck to calm these seas.

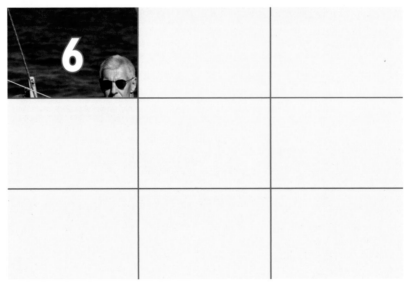

Hang Ten! Oops, Wrong Sport

It's all smiles for this snowboarding team. Could be the rose-colored glasses.

Girl Power

We may have switched things up, but we committed no errors.

Like Mother, Like Daughter

Find the eleven changes we've made to this ski outing, then meet us at the bottom of the bunny slope.

Holy Mole

We've chopped up these tamales and stirred up the pieces. Can you pull the ingredients together?

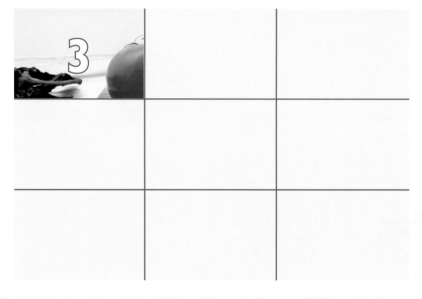

Wheeeeee!

Kick-flip your observation skills and you'll skate through this puzzle in no time.

What's Cooking?

The menu has changed at this family gathering. Pull up a chair and feast your eyes.

Two-Wheeler

You won't get far on this antique. Put on your spectacles and find the ten changes we've made to this prickly scene.

Burgers and Dogs

Plenty of American favorites are on this picnic table. Are you a mustard or ketchup person?

Red or Green?

Help these learners get back to school by checking our work and finding the differences.

○ ○ ○ ○ ○ ○ ○ ○ ○ ○ | **10** CHANGES

White Water, White Knuckles

Can you navigate this puzzle and find
the one picture that veers slightly off course?

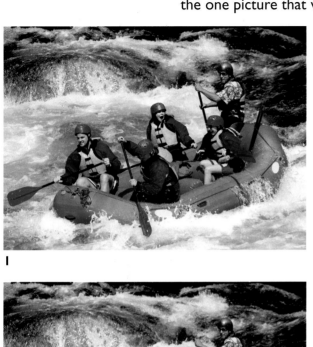

1

2

3

4

5

6

DASTARDLY

Butterflies Are Free

But some of these beauties might be a bit imbalanced.

Good Knight!

In which picture has one of these riders
undergone a slight wardrobe change?

1

2

3

4

5

6

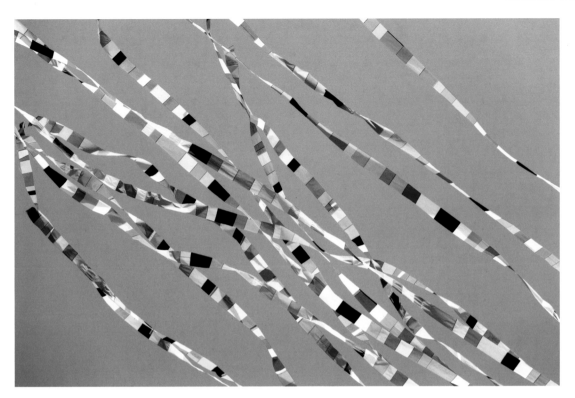

Ribbons in the Sky

This scene looks serene but closer inspection will reveal some chaos in the friendly sky.

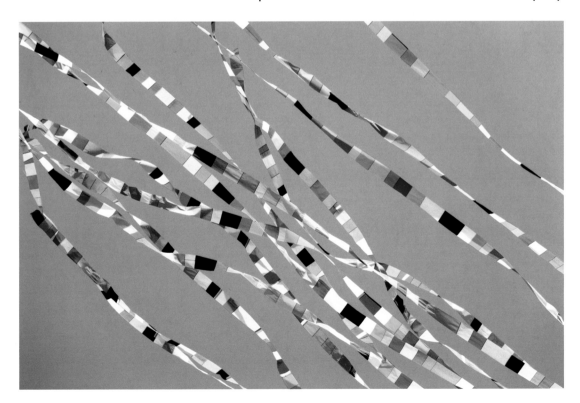

Knock, Knock

The moon might be full by the time you solve this puzzle.

Java Jump Start

Wake up and find the sixteen changes at this coffee bar.

Sugar Overload

Reward yourself with cake after finding the differences sprinkled throughout this puzzle.

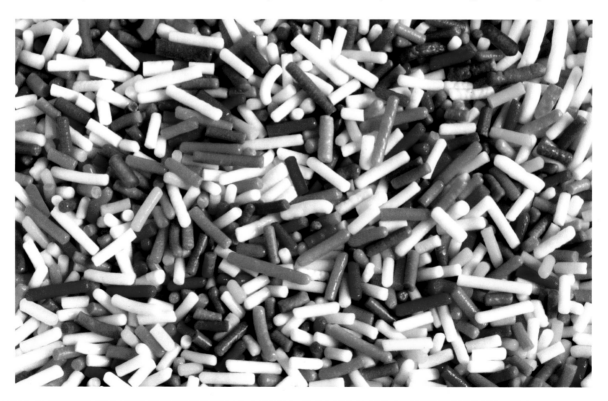

Canine Resort

This Mexican trip could be a boon*dogg*le, but how would we know?
At least our furry friend brought along sun protection.

My Sweet Babushka

These dolls aren't hiding anything. Everything is in plain view if you look close enough.

Antique Shop

Finding the differences here could take longer than it takes to churn cream into butter.

Spectacular Display

You may need an extra pair of eyes to find the unique bird in this sextet.

1

2

3

4

5

6

Smiley Faces

Stop clowning around and solve this puzzle.

Bedroom Bedlam

We'd scream, too. Better pencil in some cleanup time, little lady.

Abstract Hardware

Is your brain hardwired for this?

Between a Rock and a Hard Place

You're not the only pebble on the beach, but you may be the only hope for this pile of rubble.

Piece This

In more ways than one, these quilt pieces are quite busy.

Off the Hook

We're angling to tie you in knots with this puzzle. Will you be lured by the colorful bait?

Here's One for the Books

Pore through the stacks and you'll find we've made some binding changes.

Gone to Pot

We've smashed up this pretty pottery. Can you pick up the pieces?

"Throw Me Something, Mister!"

Draw a bead on these shenanigans to find the mischief our revelers have made.

Knitter's Paradise

Knitters love their craft and that's no yarn. Can you stitch together
the ten differences between these two pictures?

Junkyard Gnome

You'll need a sharp eye to dig through the nuts and bolts of this puzzle.

TGIF!

These revelers are ready for the weekend. Which party did we crash?

1

2

3

4

5

6

Moroccan Mania

Bizarre things are happening at the shoe bazaar. Can you bring this market back to normal?

Shell Game

Who sells seashells by the seashore? We don't know.
But we do know this puzzle is no day at the beach.

Neighborhood Nonsense

Our hat is off to you if you can spot all the renovations that have altered this colorful corner.

The License Plate Game

Put these plates in order and you'll find out which state you
can claim in our version of the license plate game.

"Oh, You Shouldn't Have!"

But since you did, find the fourteen alterations we've
made to this pile of presents, and let's wrap this up.

SOLUTION KEY

PAGE **4**

PAGE **5**

PAGE **6**

PAGE **7**

PAGE **8**

PAGE **10**

PAGE 11

PAGE 12

PAGE 13

PAGE 14

PAGE 16

PAGE 17

PAGE 18

PAGE 20

PAGE 21

PAGE 22

PAGE 23

PAGE 24

PAGE 26

PAGE 27

PAGE 28

PAGE 29

PAGE 30

PAGE 32

PAGE **33**

PAGE **36**

PAGE **38**

PAGE **39**

PAGE **40**

PAGE **41**

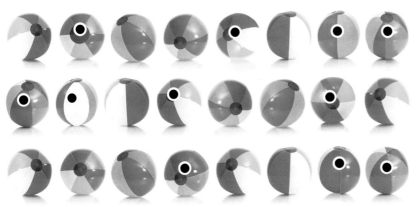

PAGE **42**

PAGE **43**

PAGE **44**

PAGE **45**

PAGE **46**

PAGE **47**

PAGE **48**

PAGE **50**

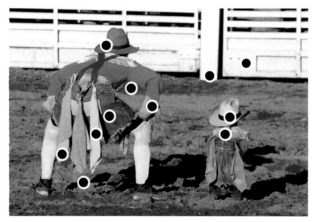

PAGE **51**

PAGE **52**

PAGE **53**

PAGE **54**

PAGE 56

| 5 | 8 | 3 | 6 |
| 1 | 4 | 2 | 7 |

PAGE 58

PAGE 59

PAGE 60

AGE 62

PAGE 63

PAGE **64**

PAGE **65**

PAGE **66**

PAGE **68**

PAGE **69**

PAGE **70**

PAGE **72**

PAGE **73**

PAGE **74**

PAGE **76**

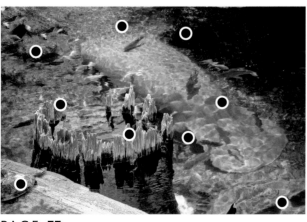

PAGE **77**

PAGE **78**

PAGE **80**

PAGE **81**

PAGE **82**

PAGE **83**

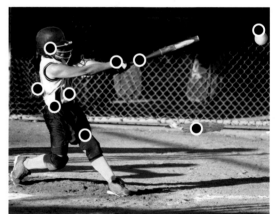

PAGE **84**

PAGE **85**

PAGE **86**

PAGE **87**

PAGE **88**

PAGE **89**

PAGE **90**

PAGE **92**

PAGE **93**

PAGE **96**

PAGE **98**

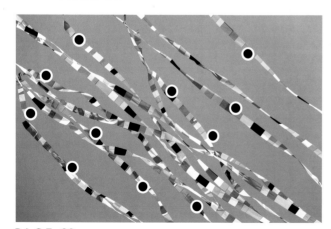

PAGE **99**

PAGE **100**

PAGE 102

PAGE 104

PAGE 105

PAGE 106

PAGE 108

PAGE 110

USA TODAY.

PAGE 111

PAGE 112

PAGE 114

PAGE 116

PAGE 117

PAGE 118

PAGE **120**

PAGE **122**

PAGE **123**

PAGE **124**

PAGE **126**

PAGE **128**

PAGE 129

PAGE 130

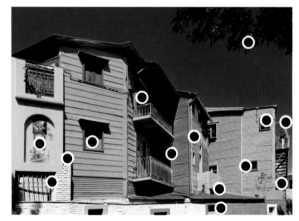

PAGE 132

PAGE 133

PAGE 134

Photo Credits

All photos © iStockphoto.com/Marcela Barsse, page 4; Judy Barranco, page 5; Sam Lee, page 6; Teresa Guerrero, page 7; Steven Allan, page 8; John Woodworth, page 10; Jill Chen, page 11; webphotographeer, page 12; Don Wilkie, page 13; Linda Macpherson, page 14; pxlar8, page 16; Nathan Gutshall-Kresge, page 17; Gaby Jalbert, page 18; Morganl, page 20; Pathathai Chungyam, page 21; Captured Nuance, page 22; Jani Bryson, page 23; Jane Norton, page 24; Mehmet Salih Guler, page 26; Volker Kreinacke, page 27; Gina Smith, page 28; Sami Suni, page 29; Juan Monino, page 30; Trevor Fisher, page 32; james steidl, page 33; Jeremy Richards, page 36; Tom Hahn, page 38; Gene Chutka, page 39; Meppu, page 40; Jamie Wilson, page 41; Sean Locke, page 42; JackJelly, page 43; Lise Gagne, page 44; Cheryl Casey, page 45; Alexander Hafemann, page 46; PhotographerOlympus, page 47; Ben Taylor, page 48; sx70, page 50; Diane Garcia, page 51; ShyMan, page 52; eROMAZe, page 53; John Peacock, page 54; Erik de Graaf, page 56; cjmckendry, page 58; Michelle Milliman, page 59; Sean Locke, page 60; Brasil2, page 62; kutay tanir, page 63; Jason Lugo, page 64; Yvonne Chamberlain, page 65; Brad Wieland, page 66; Ekaterina Monakhova, page 68; alphavisions, page 69; Terry Alexander, page 70; Robert Bremec, page 72; Andresr, page 73; Jani Bryson, page 74; Verena Matthew, page 76; Stephen Meese, page 77; Olga Lyubkina, page 78; Randolph Jay Braun, page 80; Jamie Carroll, page 81; Monika Lewandowska, page 82; Vladimir Piskunov, page 83; Iris Nieves, page 84; Doug Berry, page 85; Lori Martin, page 86; Christian Carroll, page 87; Sean Locke, page 88; EveStock, page 89; Rob Belknap, page 90; Sean Locke, page 92; Ben Blankenburg, page 93; Ismael Montero Verdu, page 96; Jacqui Dunster, page 98; Massimo Merlini, page 99; Carmen Martínez Banús, page 100; Tuyen Nguyen, page 102; Marie-france Bélanger, page 104; Dennis Guyitt, page 105; sarit saliman, page 106; Lee Torrens, page 108; Michael Klenetsky, page 110; Josef Philipp, page 111; Mark Rose, page 112; Konstantin Inozemtsev, page 114; webphotographeer, page 116; Emilia Kun, page 117; Chris Fertnig, page 118; Shawn Gearhart, page 120; narvikk, page 122; Dswebb, page 123; Les Palenik, page 124; Joe Cicak, page 126; Jacob Wackerhausen, page 128; Frank Rotthaus, page 129; Jonas Engström, page 130; Nikada, page 132; Craig Barhorst, page 133; Christine Balderas, page 134